U.S. HISTORY
★★★
IN REVIEW

MW00513581

THE AMERICAN REVOLUTION

SADIE SILVA

Enslow
PUBLISHING

Please visit our website, www.enslow.com. For a free color catalog of all our high-quality books, call toll free 1-800-398-2504 or fax 1-877-980-4454.

Library of Congress Cataloging-in-Publication Data

Names: Silva, Sadie, author.
Title: The American Revolution / Sadie Silva.
Description: Buffalo, New York : Enslow Publishing, [2023] | Series: U.S. history in review | Includes index.
Identifiers: LCCN 2022020888 (print) | LCCN 2022020889 (ebook) | ISBN 9781978529007 (library binding) | ISBN 9781978528987 (paperback) | ISBN 9781978529014 (ebook)
Subjects: LCSH: United States–History–Revolution, 1775-1783–Juvenile literature.
Classification: LCC E208 .S55 2023 (print) | LCC E208 (ebook) | DDC 973.3–dc23/eng/20220428
LC record available at https://lccn.loc.gov/2022020888
LC ebook record available at https://lccn.loc.gov/2022020889

Published in 2023 by
Enslow Publishing
2544 Clinton Street
Buffalo, NY 14224

Copyright © 2023 Enslow Publishing

Portions of this work were originally authored by Peter Castellano and published as *The American Revolution*. All new material this edition authored by Sadie Silva.

Designer: Leslie Taylor
Editor: Caitlin McAneney

Photo credits: Cover https://commons.wikimedia.org/wiki/File:Surrender_of_Lord_Cornwallis.jpg; series art (grunge flag) Andrey Kuzmin/Shutterstock.com; series art (stamp icon) Stocker_team/Shutterstock.com; series art (font) santstock/Shutterstock.com; p. 5 (illustration) Everett Collection/Shutterstock.com; p. 5 (map) https://commons.wikimedia.org/wiki/File:The_XIII_Colonies_1664-1783.jpg; p. 7 https://commons.wikimedia.org/wiki/File:Patrick_Henry_MET_DT9295.jpg; p. 8 https://commons.wikimedia.org/wiki/File:O!_the_fatal_Stamp.jpg; p. 9 North Wind Picture Archives/Alamy.com; p. 10 Everett Collection/Shutterstock.com; p. 11 https://commons.wikimedia.org/wiki/File:Boston_Tea_Party_Currier_colored.jpg; p. 13 https://commons.wikimedia.org/wiki/File:Flickr_-_USCapitol_-_The_First_Continental_Congress,_1774.jpg; p. 15 (top) Jorge Salcedo/Shutterstock.com; p. 15 (bottom) https://commons.wikimedia.org/wiki/File:Midnight_Ride_of_Paul_Revere_by_Edward_Mason_Eggleston.jpg; p. 17 https://www.shutterstock.com/image-illustration/john-hancock-signs-declaration-independence-1776-238067902; p. 19 https://commons.wikimedia.org/wiki/File:The_Death_of_General_Warren_at_the_Battle_of_Bunker%27s_Hill.jpg; p. 20 https://commons.wikimedia.org/wiki/File:Fort_Ticonderoga_1775.jpg; p. 21 https://commons.wikimedia.org/wiki/File:Washington_Crossing_the_Delaware_by_Emanuel_Leutze,_MMA-NYC,_1851.jpg; p. 23 Everett Collection/Shutterstock.com; p. 25 Patrick Breig/Shutterstock.com; p. 27 Everett Collection/Shutterstock.com; p. 28 Nicolas Raymond/Shutterstock.com; p. 29 https://commons.wikimedia.org/wiki/File:PreliminaryTreatyOfParisPainting.jpg.

All rights reserved. No part of this book may be reproduced in any form without permission in writing from the publisher, except by a reviewer.

Printed in the United States of America

CPSIA compliance information: Batch #CWENS23: For further information, contact Enslow Publishing, New York, New York, at 1-800-398-2504.

Find us on

Contents

Words in the glossary appear in **bold** the
first time they are used in the text.

From Colonies to Country

Without the American Revolution, the United States wouldn't **exist**. The country grew out of 13 British **colonies**. Some colonists thought Great Britain was treating them unfairly. They thought Great Britain taxed colonists unfairly. They had no say in British government.

Learn More

Loyalists were colonists who were loyal, or true, to Great Britain. Patriots were colonists who wanted to fight against Great Britain.

13 Original Colonies

THE
XIII COLONIES
1664-1783.

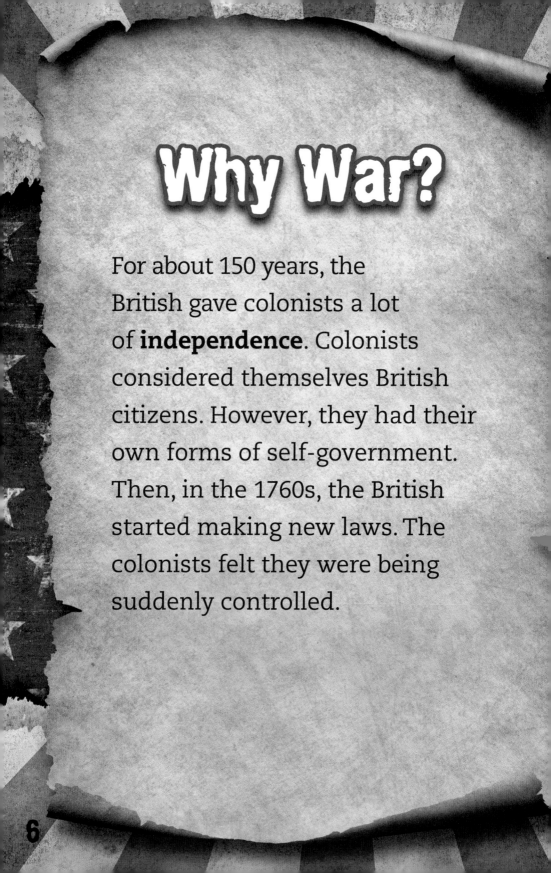

Why War?

For about 150 years, the British gave colonists a lot of **independence**. Colonists considered themselves British citizens. However, they had their own forms of self-government. Then, in the 1760s, the British started making new laws. The colonists felt they were being suddenly controlled.

Patrick Henry's "Liberty or Death" speech before the Virginia Assembly

Patrick Henry

PROCEEDINGS OF THE Virginia Assembly

Learn More

Colonies had groups of local **representatives** called assemblies that made local laws. However, the laws had to follow British orders.

From 1754 to 1763, Great Britain fought against France on North American land. It was called the French and Indian War. To pay for it, Great Britain taxed its colonists. Many colonists believed they shouldn't be taxed without having representatives in the British government.

Learn More

In 1764, the Sugar Act taxed sugar. In 1765, the Stamp Act taxed newspapers, cards, and more. The Townshend Acts of 1767 taxed glass, paper, and tea.

Stamp Act revolt

In 1770, British soldiers fired on a group of colonists. Five colonists died. The colonists called it the Boston **Massacre**. In 1773, the Tea Act gave the British East India Company control of all tea trade in the colonies. **Tensions** worsened.

the Boston Massacre

Learn More

Unhappy with the Tea Act, a group of colonists dumped tea into Boston Harbor. This is called the Boston Tea Party.

the Boston Tea Party

The First Continental Congress

The passage of the Intolerable Acts (1774) was the last straw. This group of laws closed Boston Harbor. They placed Massachusetts under more British control. This caused 12 of the 13 colonies to meet for the First Continental Congress. It met in Philadelphia, Pennsylvania.

Learn More

The First Continental Congress wanted to push back against British laws. It called for colonists to boycott, or stop buying, British goods.

This Means War

Patriots in Massachusetts became more and more upset by the spring of 1775. Some gathered arms and began training for war. On April 19, 1775, the British army arrived in the Massachusetts towns of Lexington and Concord. A shot was fired—and battle broke out.

Paul Revere

Learn More

On April 18, 1775, Paul Revere was one of those sent to deliver the news that the British were heading to Lexington and Concord. The British wanted to take patriot leaders and arms.

No Path to Peace

In May 1775, the Second Continental Congress met with representatives from all 13 colonies. They formed the Continental army. George Washington was its commander, or leader. They sent the Olive Branch Petition to British King George III. It asked for a peaceful solution. He didn't answer.

signing the Declaration of Independence, 1776

Learn More

The Declaration of Independence was written during the Second Continental Congress. It stated that the 13 British colonies would be one free nation.

Bloody Battles

The colonists had declared independence. However, a war still had to be fought. In June 1775, the patriots' forces lost the Battle of Bunker Hill. However, many British soldiers died in the battle, which made the patriots feel they had a chance.

Learn More

Much of the fighting took place in the northern colonies during the first few years. The British forces had a strong navy, which helped them succeed early on.

Battle of Bunker Hill, 1775

The patriots took Fort Ticonderoga in New York in May 1775. It was a **stronghold** for them until 1777. American patriots had another success in December 1776 when the Continental army stormed a British post in Trenton, New Jersey.

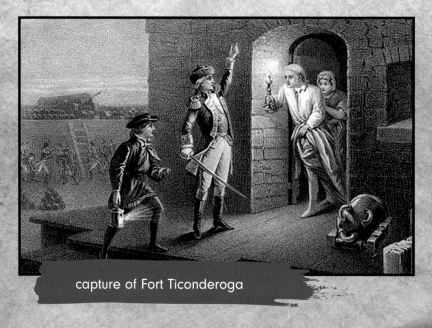

capture of Fort Ticonderoga

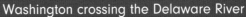

Washington crossing the Delaware River

Learn More

On Christmas night 1776, General George Washington brought 5,400 troops across the Delaware River. They surprise-attacked **Hessian** forces in Trenton.

Setbacks and Success

The Continental army faced many setbacks. Troops spent the winter of 1777 to 1778 at Valley Forge in Pennsylvania. Many men died of illness and dealt with hunger. The British continued to succeed in battle. Luckily, the Battle of Saratoga in 1777 was a turning point.

Valley Forge, 1777

Learn More

On October 17, 1777, the Continental army won the Second Battle of Saratoga in New York. This made other countries believe the patriots' cause wasn't impossible.

Friends with the French

In 1778, France signed a **treaty** to help the colonists as an **ally**. France sent thousands of soldiers to fight. The Marquis de Lafayette is the most famous French soldier who fought in the American Revolution. He became a good friend to George Washington.

statue of the Marquis de Lafayette (left) and George Washington (right)

Learn More France had already been quietly giving the Continental army money and arms. The treaty made the alliance official.

Surrender at Yorktown

With help from France, the Continental army had new fighting power. Continental army leaders used new **tactics** and began to beat British forces. They forced the British general, Lord Charles Cornwallis, to **surrender** at Yorktown, Virginia, on October 18, 1781.

Learn More

The Battle of Yorktown trapped the British army. They were surrounded by land and sea. It was the last major battle of the American Revolution.

Cornwallis

surrender of General Cornwallis

Independence at Last

Fighting ended in 1781. However, the war wasn't officially over until 1783. That's when the American colonies and Great Britain signed the Treaty of Paris. The former colonies were now an independent nation. The United States of America was born.

Signing the Treaty of Paris, 1783

Learn More

The American Revolution sparked revolutions around the world, such as in France, Haiti, and Ireland.

Timeline

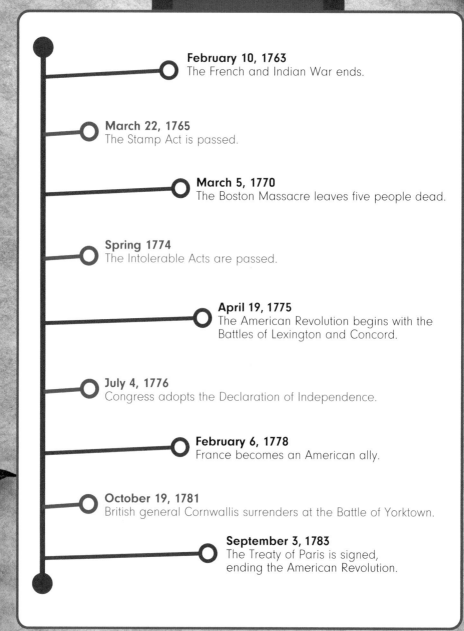

February 10, 1763
The French and Indian War ends.

March 22, 1765
The Stamp Act is passed.

March 5, 1770
The Boston Massacre leaves five people dead.

Spring 1774
The Intolerable Acts are passed.

April 19, 1775
The American Revolution begins with the Battles of Lexington and Concord.

July 4, 1776
Congress adopts the Declaration of Independence.

February 6, 1778
France becomes an American ally.

October 19, 1781
British general Cornwallis surrenders at the Battle of Yorktown.

September 3, 1783
The Treaty of Paris is signed, ending the American Revolution.

Glossary

ally: One of two or more people or groups who work together.

colony: A piece of land under the control of another country.

exist: To be.

Hessian: Describing German soldiers who fought for the British in the American Revolution.

independence: Freedom from outside control.

massacre: The killing of a large number of people, especially when they cannot guard themselves.

representative: One who stands for a group of people.

stronghold: A place that has been strengthened, especially in case of an attack.

surrender: To give up.

tactic: A way of accomplishing a military aim.

tension: Pressure or strain between people or things.

treaty: An agreement between countries.

For More Information

Books

Abramson, Marcia. *The Declaration of Independence.* Minneapolis, MN: Bearport Publishing Company, 2021.

Vink, Amanda. *Team Time Machine Crosses the Delaware.* New York, NY: Gareth Stevens Publishing, 2020.

Websites

American Revolution
www.dkfindout.com/us/history/american-revolution/
Discover more about the American Revolution.

Publisher's note to educators and parents: Our editors have carefully reviewed these websites to ensure that they are suitable for students. Many websites change frequently, however, and we cannot guarantee that a site's future contents will continue to meet our high standards of quality and educational value. Be advised that students should be closely supervised whenever they access the internet.

Index